THE ADVANCE THEORY OF MOMENTUM

SOMETHING THAT WORLD DON'T KNOW

HITEN YADAV

Copyright © Hiten Yadav
All Rights Reserved.

This book has been published with all efforts taken to make the material error-free after the consent of the author. However, the author and the publisher do not assume and hereby disclaim any liability to any party for any loss, damage, or disruption caused by errors or omissions, whether such errors or omissions result from negligence, accident, or any other cause.

While every effort has been made to avoid any mistake or omission, this publication is being sold on the condition and understanding that neither the author nor the publishers or printers would be liable in any manner to any person by reason of any mistake or omission in this publication or for any action taken or omitted to be taken or advice rendered or accepted on the basis of this work. For any defect in printing or binding the publishers will be liable only to replace the defective copy by another copy of this work then available.

To My Parents, Friends, teachers, My dear hardwork and
Precious dedication

Contents

Acknowledgements

Thank you all the scientists. for all your hardwork and dedication to create all the new formulaes that is the main reason that helped me making this formulae. And I also want to dedicate this book to many scientists, physicist, mathematician and astronomers. That includes a never ending list of Honourable Srinivas Ramanujan, Sir Issac Newton, Galileo Galili, Sir Albert enistein and many more. They worked really hard to make our society modern and my harwork is nothing in front of them. And also want to thank all the teachers of my school that were always ready to motivate me and helped me a lot in this difficult journey. And My dearest parents that always supported me, no matter in which situation I am, and also all the friends of mine. I thank you all, because of you all only I am able to write my book and invent a new formulae.

I
Theme

This book is about an invention that is done by Hiten yadav. Here he tells about his whole story that, how he face many failures and overcome them with the help of his parents and teachers. This is also based on a true story of a 14 year old child. Here, Hiten is also telling us about age is just a number. And now after many failures, he succefully invented a new formulae about Momentum. In this book we can also learn basic physics like what is physics, what are different aspects and physics quantities in it and many more. And if you will read the title, it seems to be complex but when you get inside this book, you will definately understand each and every topic in it. Here about the title, the title is the name of the invention that is done by Hiten. The Message that we can learn in this book is that we will definately get success, slowly but surely. This book is not only for Academic bases, this can also be used as a self helped book.

II
Introduction

When I was in 7th class, my favourite subject would be Physics I use to told my father that "I love Physics and also, will pursue my career in that only", and then my father used to say that "Okay i agree that you love Physics but now your are only stick to your syllabus that is going on, that everyone do, what extra you are doing?" That one sentence, at first demotivated me but then i thought that my father was right, I am not doing anything extra, Everyone were studying the same course that i am doing, so what was special with me? Then with full dedication I use to think that what should i do so that i can make a difference with all my mates and with the whole world. For few days, i left everything thing, I left talking with all my friends and was isolated in my small room. Then after few weeks i got frustrated and decided to left this and live a simple life that everyone were living. Then this gone for 2 months, then i decided that not to leave Physics and do something extra other then my course and want to leave my comfort zone. But as i was a child, I don't know what to do? From where to start? And the most Importantly How to Start? Then I thought that who gave me this problem? Who made me do all of this? Yes! My Father. Then being a little innocent child, I went to my father. And then after that I went to him and asked that "Father I want to do something extra, something special that no one of my mates have done!", Then my father smile and said "Ok! So you are saying that you want me to put you in coaching so something like that?" Then I said "No,no i don't want to go there, I need to do something special!" Then my father said me to give him some time and he will tell me after a day. I agreed with this and went to sleep. After a day early in the morning with hope in eyes and smile in face, I went to my parent's room where i saw my father sleeping, I was sad at first, and then I asked my mom about this that why my father is sleeping such late, Because usually on holidays my father usually wake up on 7 AM and when i went to my parent's room it was already 8 AM, My mother said that he slept late at night and he was also thinking og something. Then I smiled of thinking that he must be thinking of some idea so that i can make a difference with my mates in school.

III

The First step

Then with an happy, innocent face I began to wait from my father to wake up and tell me about the idea that he though throughout the night. Then the clock goes to 9 AM, I saw the bedroom my father was not there then i asked my mom about my father she said "He must be in the bathroom", I nodded and again waited for about 10 minutes in hope. Now also I am that type of child that has very little patience and became extremly excited for about something that he will get or he will do. And the same goes to that time, I was becoming extremely excited to know that what my father has thought about me. So then my father came out from the bathroom, and with in a blink of eye I ran towards him with hope in eyes, and the funny part was that my father was extremely scared to saw someone rushing towards him, and there is a point in this. One must be scared to saw someone running wildly towards you. Then I asked my father "Good morning papa, have you think about something?", My Father questioned "About what,son?". I then reminded him about our conversation that happened yesterday, then he smiled and said "Yeah, yeah I have thought about that the whole night, and i have an amazing idea about that." I was extremely excited about what he is going to say, and I exclaimed "What is it dad!". Then he said that "I will only tell you in only one condition." I asked"What condition?". Then he explained "The Condition is that, you will follow this everyday and will always do this in routine. If you will promise this, then only i will tell you about that idea." I promised that as I was very desperate to listen that idea he was going to say. Then he eleaborated saying " See son now all you are doing is your course, you are only stick to your course not doing anything extra, so what i will suggest that you can complete the physics of this class quickly as you love that, so what you can do is instead of wasting your time in playing and watching t.v, you can do the physics of higher classes like of class 9 and 10th so from there you can make a difference between you and your mates, And also you know that there are many branches in physics, as you only told me that like classical physics, mechanical physics, nuclear physics, quantum physics etc... so you can choose any branch out of these and study them in dateail, I know it will be difficult for you to do these, as it now you are only in 7th grade, but if you want to achieve something you will need to do some sacrifices." I actually was agreeing with my dad about this, and agreed with his idea. And then i thought a lot about this and I also have questions regarding this that 'How to start?', 'From where to start?', 'When should start? With all these questions in mind, my summer holidays started of 7th, and i have pretty much free time at home and as a 7th grader I also don't have a lot of holiday homework in that. So in short i have a good time to start and also with the permission of my parents I also ordered some book of 9th and 10th, so i could get some guidence from them. And I was also pretty much excited to start and also to show off with my friends and mates, that "*I am so good at physics that i have started it of higher classes like 9th and 10th*". So then after 3-4 days of summer holidays the books that i have ordered were arrived at my home and I have pretty excited to start. And now also, you must be thinking that, the title of the book is something else but from now I am just talking about something completely else from the title, so I request you to please wait, will definately tell you about this about some time. So now let's get back to the story, I was pretty much excited to start and the first chapter that i open was from class 9th physics which was '**MOTION**'. And at first I was not understanding a single word from it, but luckily we are living in the modern word, so I can take help from internet easily. And in my home we have well internet facilities, so after continuos try and with full dedication I was slowly, but was able to understand some of the topic of higher classes physics.

IV

The Sad part....

I was very happy as I was understanding some concepts clearly and,want to learn more and more. My curiosity of Physics was increasing day by day and want to continue this. But there was also a sad part about this, in a day i used to study around 3-4 hours, which was quite good for a 7th grader. But the problem is I was almost only studying Physcs and a little bit of mathematics. I was also only studying maths only because there are some topics in Physics also that if you need to study them, you need to know some maths. But I don't care about this I only was caring about Physics. And guess what, my grades also were coming tremendousely down as I was not focussig on any other subject. My Parents were extremely dissapointed and worried about my performance. My Grades were good in Science and Maths but was below average in all other subjects. So, My Parents called me and asked that "What is happening with you?" I politely questioned that "What you all are saying? What is the problem?" They were saying that your grades are continuously going down and your performance is also deproved as you were earlier, What is the reason, you can explain us son. Then I told them that "Mummy, Papa I have left studying any of the subjects except Physics and Maths, I have a lot of interest in Physics that's why I am not able to focus on any of the subjects other then Physics. And till now I have done many of the topic of Higher classes of this subject. My Mother asked me "Son, who has given you this idea?" I pointing out my father "Papa has given me this idea to study the physics of higher classes." Then my Father said "Yeah.. I have given you this idea but I don't want you to only focus in Physics, you only need to focus on other subjects like Hindi, English etc." So then I asked in a sad tone "What do you mean, I should not focuus on Physics and just focus on my course and my syllabus?" Then they smiled and said "No, no We don't mean this, we are saying that you can do this, what you are doing but you should also focus on your syllabus that is going on, And then you can do this as a hobby." I at first like this idea but has many questions regarding this like 'How much time should I give to this' 'Will i be able to handle the pressure of all subjects with this additional hobby' So i asked this to my parents and they also answer these questions and that helped me today also. By seeing my parents tips you can also manage time easily So here's my parents answer , "Hmm.. so you have a problem with time management, you are not able to manage the time. So, what you can do is you can devote around 30 minutes on it per day, and for different subjects you can denote them different time as per yoour choice. As Science and maths is your strong subjects, yoou can understandf much more in very little time, so you must give them a little less time as compared to other subjects so you can give them each 45 minutes per day and as per we know your hindi is not that much good, so you must give that a little bit more time as it is your weak point." So this thing actually worked I was able to manage My hobby with my school studies.

V

The Disappointment and The Frustration

After I was doing my work or hobby with my syllabus, I was able to do questions of 10th and 11th, when I was in class 8 and slowly slowly, I was getting bored of this. I thought that what if i finished the syllabus of whole 12th, then what will I do. This i don't want to discuss with my parents as they will also get bored of it and will also scold me of not focussing on my syllabus instead of thinking about this. And I was also feeling lucky that I have such type of supportive parents (Not in a sarcastic way, really they both have supported me in my difficult times. Like If i got low grades or if i need some consultency they act like they are my friends so I can talk to them freely). Now I started thinking what to do, and for few days I was also not doing any kind of physics. And also my 8th was also going to be end within few weeks. So my plan was that, I will thought of an idea in these few weeks and then will implement it when I will be in 9th, as simple as that. But it was not as it was shown. It was extremely difficult for me to think of an idea and also it must be a practical one. Then at the end of the week my 9th was going to start, and also i was extremely frustrated that i have wasted 3 weeks, just not doing anything. Then an amazing idea occur to me, what happened was my mother said to me that you must play with your friends as holidays are going on and then your 9th will start from the next week, so you must enjoy these days. I agreed with this and went to streets and on the 3rd day when we were playing there was one of my friend batting, and I was the one bowling then I bowl him and he played a shot that we have not seen somewhere, it was an absolutely new shot that we have ever seen. Then me and my friends asked the batsman that how did you do this, his name was sandeep and he said that he also did'nt know that how does he made that shot, then one of my friends said that he has invented this shot. And that line spark me in my head and I have an amazing idea. I immediately left the match and went to my home saying that I have an headache, and immediately wrrote that idea in my small diary, as i was forgot things quite early. Then i was extremely happy that after few days of dissapointment and frustration, I was able to get and idea.

VI
Failures

Then I have everything going with my plan, and also told my plan to my parents and they were also happy to know this and everything was gooing according to my plan. And then I was extremely happy and was enjoying each and every moment of that 3 days left holidays. As I knew that then at 9th I will fully focus on this idea that I have got. And then my 9th started and now i don't want to make the mistake that i have made earlier, I was managing my time like a pro only because of my parents tip and also I have enough knowledge of physics so that I can invent a formulae or A Theory. And I started, and as I was totally new in this field i don't have an idea how to do this. Now also, I used to laugh that how i made formulaes at that time, I think you all will also laugh at me after hearing this. What i used to do is just cross multiply the formulaes that exist and then named it that this is my new owned formulae. Like there are 2 formulaes a=b/c and the other one is d=e/ a, these are just examples, so what I do that time was just cross multiply the formulae like putting the value of b/c (which is a) in the second formulae, that becomes d=e/b/c or d=ec/b, so here it is our brand new formulae. I know i was quite studpid at that time. And again I took this too far, what i do was with the same method I created a formulae, let's just say it Formulae A and went to my teacher saying that I have invented a new formulae, and with that I wasted a lot of time of her. After that she explained me how these things worked, and I feel extremely embaresed in front of her. But she instead of scolding me for wasting her time in this, she praised me that I have done a great thing and I should continue this. But I was at the same time feeling fulling frustrated and demotivated as I have done a lot of hardwork, I have literally spent more than a month in this stupid formulae. Then i consulted with my counceller teacher and she literally motivated me a lot. With this, I understand that failures are also important part of life and I will face a lot of failures in my whole life. Then I again started with my work and make another formulae and now also i still remember that I created a formulae of Gravitation, It is not the exact formulae of Gravitation but we can see it is the postulate of it. To all my dear readers, who don't know what gravitation is so, Gravitaion is a type of invisible force that have a tendency to attract something only in one condition if it have mass. So anything that have mass attract something. Like Sun attracts earth, but earth does not attract sun, Why?, because the more the mass the more the gravitational force. So as we all know that sun has more mass then earth so it also have more Gravitational force, So this is what gravitation is so this is exactly what I gave a theory on and then I also talked about this with my Science teacher and then also she said that the way you have don4e is absolutely correct but, unfortunately it is already invented by Sir Issac Newton 356 and he already has given the law of gravitatiion, the I asked my teacher that "Mam but my law is completely different from Law of gravitration." and then she said that "See my child! This is what called as modified version of something" I asked "Mam could you please elaborate it?" Then my teacher said "See there is someone who discovered something, so to make it is our scientist modified the version to make this easier for common people to understand. So that is what you have made!" So then I laughed and said "So teacher, do you mean that if i would been have born 3 century's earlier or to be exact 356 years earlier then i could have been true!" And the she replied with a laugh and our conversation ended. Now you must have seen a difference between the first Hiten that was failed and the next Hiten that have failed, both have reaceived the same thing "*Failure*" but there reaction were absolutely different from each other. So I have learnt a lot of things from my first mistake, not only in making of a formulae but also in the psychology of failure. So I will suggest you that failure is a part of life that every have weather in career, family, or anything we will definately receive that. And some people get used to it in the first try and some need time to become used to it. And we need to learn things from our own failures rather then becoming sad and dissapointed. 'By failing we are one step closer to succes'. And now also I am in 10th and my failures have taught me a lot about life and most importantely about myself. And after that also I have failed many times, but instead of becoming frustrated and sad and I learn from them and try again.

VII

The Taste of succes

As, I have tries a lot and failed a lot of times, I always learnt from them and try again in the formulae. And there were a lot of problems when yoou are trying to invent something new . And when I was trying about these I also have a question 'Which is the part of physics that is very less covered and have least invention'. So for this answer also there is a story. So due to the COVID-19 pandemic our classes were going online and i still remember the chapter that was going on in science was of Physics annd the name of the chapter is 'Force and laws of motion' and the topic that was going on was of momentum. And I have a habit of asking a lots of doubts, so I my science teacher and she knows that I was trying to invent something and asked her "Mam, what actually is is momentum, Can i feel it, as i can fell the force, I can feel time is going, I can feel someone is putting physicsal pressure on me, so why can't I feel momentum." Then she answered my question by saying "Hiten, the all we know about momentum is that it is the measure of quantity of motion, except this we know nothing much about it." So I thanked my teacher for clearing my doubt and actually this answer attracted me towards momentum to know much more about it and i get to know that we only know that momentum is only mass*velocity. Then I thought why can't I work on Momentum, there is also not many things invented in it. Then I started researching and learning more and more about momentum in depth and my previous higher level knowledge also helped me in it. And I also took help from my Science teacher to learn more about this and also discussed this with my parents. They were also happy, that i am putting my efforts in a good thing. I don't bother about the result, I was happy that I am doing something extra then others. And then I also realized that I am not doing this to show-off, bbut I am doing this for my own good, to enhance my knowledge. Then I started working on momentum, and I know slowly but surely I will definately be able to get succes in my work. And the one and only thing that I don't want to do is, to not give up. And I will also suggest my dear readers please don't give up in your life, if you are failing in something, be happy because you are 1 more step closer to succes. And the one thing that i can guarentee is that if you will never give up, you will definately be succesfull in whatever you are doing. I also remember the story regarding this, maybe yoou have read this. There is a village and there used to live an old man and the villagers used to say that if this old man started dancing no matter how much sunlight is there, it started raining. So 4 well educated students challenged the old man that they can also do this, So the 1st student started dancing and after 45 minutes of continuous dancing he gave up. Then the 2nd student came and he also of continuous dancing of 30 minutes he gave up. The same also goes with the rest of the 2 students, they danced for 30-40 minutes and the they gave up. Then the old man started dancing, and he continuosly danced for 1 hour nothing happend then 2 hours passed, nothing happen and then finally in the evening of after continuous dancing of 8 hours, it started pouring heavily. All the 4 students were shocked and they apologized to the old man and asked him "How did you do this?" Then the old man smiled and answer "When I am going to dance,I think of only one thing that I will not stop till it rains." So with this short story there is a deep message hidden. We should not gie up until, we achieved to our goal. And actually this story motivated me a lot, in overcoming my frustration after my failures. Then I started working on Momentum and I thought of many previous formulaes through which I can take help from it and make my own formulae. And then after many failures and hardwork of 6 months I finally was able to Invent a whole new formulae and checked everything like "Is it invented by anyone else in the world?" or "Is it a postulate of some other formulae?" as I have done this mistake earlier and I also checked that is it available in internet or not. And luckily it was neither invented and nor it is a postulated of any other formulae and to my shock it was also neither in Internet. And I also discussed with my teacher and she was also not aware of it.So then I got to know that I have really invented something. But there was a problem I have discovered something new in the field of physics but I don't know how to publish it as my parents also don't have enough knowledge in this field. So I only need to do something for my formulae. Then I talked to some of my friends that what to do and take consent with my elders. So most of them were suggesting only 1 thing that I should patent my work as early as possible. And I also like that idea, so as it is 21st century, we all are surrounded by internet., and if we will see it in a good way it can help us a lot in our life. So I search many of the patent companies and contacted them. And within few days I received a lot of mails and phone calls regarding my patent and I told them that I have invented a new formulae in the field of physics which is completely new and I want to patent it. And I discuss this with more then 5 companies and they all give me the same answer that "This is a scientific research and this cannot be patented, there are some rules to patent something, and there is one rule in India that you cannot invent any scientific research." So I asked them about any solution and out of 6 only 2 gave me the solution, the rest of 4 just say "We actually don't have any knowledge regarding this, we know that you can figure it out." So the rest of 2 patent agents gave me 2 solutions, the first one said that "There is a rule to patent something and it is that it must make things easier for common people, they must get any advantage with it, so as per your forumlae they are not getting any advantage with it, so if you can manage to make anything that can be made in industries and is able to make profit by selling , you can come again to us and we will defdinately patent it." And the second patent agent told me that "It is true that you cannot patent it but this does not mean that your work is a waste, what you can do is you can wrote a book or an article or something like that, So that the whole world will know that you have invented something, and I am prety sure that you know who is Albert einstein and Sir Issac newton, they have also not patented them, what they have done is they have wrote a book regarding this and published it and then they got famous overnight because of there work, I think you can do this." So again I got a failure, but at the same time I was also relaxed that I have 2 solution, my work is not a waste.So at that time I thought that I need to go with the 1st solution as I have literally no knowledge of how to wrote a book, and if i will go to the 1st one patent agents can also help me but if I will go to the 2nd one no one will be there to assist me and at the end I am also a small teenager. Then for assistence I also took help from my mother, oh sorry I forgot to introduce my parents, yeah I know it's quite late. My Mother's name is Poonam and my father's name is Raj kumar. And my mother is a housewife and my father is the one who earn for our living. Yeah, so where I am, I took advice from my parents and then they also told me that you should go to the 1st solution. Then I started working for the first solution and thoguhtfor almost 1 month that what can I do with this. But unfortunately I don't have any solution except 1 or 2 that were no realistic. Like 'Can I make a time machine with this?' I know it is kinda stupid but maybe.. you will get it later. So I was literally do not know what to do and my class 9th mid term exams were also very near. So what I decided to leave this thing for some days and focus on my exams. Then I don't know why these some days become some weeks and then some months. I was literally forgot about this formulae thing and just living a boring life. Then one day my father told me that "Hey, have you forgotten about your formulae! You have just tasted the success and you were so near to it." So I told my dad that "Papa, I am not able to find anything, I don't know that how can I made something from this and patent it and made that in a buisness?" So then my father replied "So I think the patent agents told you about the 2 solutions so what about the 2nd one, you must try it out!" I said my father "Let it be dad, I will not be able to wrote a whole book,I am not able to frame sentences, how can I wrote a whole book of thousands of words." Then he said that "You must try it out instead of wating time, remeber the promise that you have made it to me, you will never give up and always spennt some time on your formulae." but i was completely broken inside that I will not be able to do anything. But at some point my dad was saying right I can try because no one knows what can happen. So with the help of internet, I got knowledge about how to write a book and as I belongs to a middle class family, I cannot spend a single piece of note on it, I must do it for free, then I got to know about notionpress and now here I am writing a book. And now I thank god for giving me such a blessing by giving me such supportive parents.

VIII

The Advance theory of Momentum

So, this is the result of my endless tries and dedication. I have worked extremely hard to reach this conclusion. I have done endless sacrifices and with the support of my parents,teachers and friends, I am able to invent something. So now i will tell what exactly is "The Advance theory of Momentum". So this is a formulae that tells us the relation between Momentum with force, displacement/distance and with the velocity. And if we will modify it we can also create the relation of momentum with mass and time also. So you must have a lot of questions like 'Why is this so much special' 'Is there any formulae of it?' 'Is it new in the field of physics?', so now I will answer all your questions. And also now you also will have many questions regarding physics like what is momentum, what actually is force and can we feel time or is mass and weight same and what is displacement so I will explain each and every topic to you in brief. And if you are a school student this can also help you in your foundation physics. So this invention is completely new to this world and there is a lot that we can achieve from it. No one has ever invented such kind of formulae. Now you all will also have curiosty what is that formulae, so if I will tell you now I guarentee you will not understand anything unless you have learnt physics till 10th oor 11th. So I will assume that you are completely new to Physics and know almost nothing about it. So a first I will tell you what is Physics, so I will not tell you that boring definations that was taught us in our school times. So as we know there are many subjects in our world like Mathematics, English, Biology, Social studies etc etc there are many subjects so Physics is also one of them. And in our world every subject has distributed their own work. Every subject tell us something new and something different from each other. Like Maths tells us about number, arithematics and also mental discipline. Such that Physics also tells us something different. Physics tells us about How we live, about different forces,study of light, electricity, sound etc. And here every subject have different branches like in mathematics there are geometry, qlgebbra,mensuration etc and in Biology there are zoology,botany,genetics etc so in Physics also there are many branch and every branch has there own topics to study. In physics the branches are Quantum physics, Mechanics, Optics, Relativity etc. I know it is quite complex, assume that these subject are the trees and the different branches of trees are the branches of subjects and the leaves are the topics of each subject. So now why is this formulae so much special? According to me every invention in the world is special for us, as it has never came in our modern world, and obviously we can definately take some advantage and improve our society. So can we say Theory of relativity by Sir Albert einstein is not usefull for us? Absolutely not, it was a very important aspect in our today's world, even thought we common people does'nt get any advantage from it. So we should respect every invention, even thought it is small. So now step by step I will tell you each and every physical quantity and will explain it in detail so you can understand my formulae without any problem. So now I will give the list of Physical quantities that is used in my formulae. They are-

1) Force
2) Mass
3) Accelaration
4) Time
5) Momentum
6) Displacement/Distance

Force

Force is a Physical quantity in physics that was first refered by Aristotle that causes an object in 'unnatural motion'. And in common language we know force as a push or pull on something that causes a type of motion. It is a type of vector quantity. Now, if you don't know what is vector quantity, I will explai it to you. All the physical quantities in physics are of 2 types. Vector quantity and scalor quantity.. Vector quantity is a type of quantity in which direction and magnitude both matters, and whereas in scalor quantity only magnitude is the one that matters. For example- When we drive a vehicle, we go to a particular direction, it means we are accelarating to somewhere in a particular direction wher we want to go. So some physical quantity that are vector are Force, accelaratioon, velocity, dispalcacement etc. And whereas in Scalor quantity magnitude is the one that matters. For example- Let that our mass is 50 kg at India and then we move some steps towards west, so will our mass change? No, why? because Mass is a scalor quantity, direction doesn't matter in this place. So in some line I have mentioned about Newton, so what is Newton. Newton is the unit that is used to measure Force. Now you will ask, what is the need to have unit? So, if we will go to fruit seller and ask for 2 kg of apple, so in this what is kg? It is the unit that is use to measure mmass. And in our daily life it help us a lot. It would be very difficult to measure something without a unit. And now I will tell you how to calculate. So in 1686 he presented his 3 laws of motion in his book "Principia Mathematica Philosophiae Naturalis." here he has telled us a lot about force. And in his 2nd law of motion he has also given a formulae how to derive it. And that formulae is 'F=ma' where F is Force, M is Mass and A is accelaration. So from here we get to know that force is directly proptional to mass and accelaration. I request you to pls remeber it as it will help us when we will go to my formulae. And also there is a small topic about types of force. In physics for basic understanding there are 2 types of force- Contact and Non contact force. Here the name itself tells us that in Contact force there is a physical force applied with the object. Like- We push a box 2 m by putting a force of 10 N in it. So here there ia physical contact between us and the object. And the non contact force is totally opposite of contact force. Here there is no physical contact between the object and the force. Like- Electrostatic force, Magnetic force and Gravitational force. And also there is an invisible force between the Sun and earth that binds earth to rotate within the sun, and the same goes with the Earth and the moon. This Force is also known as Centripetal force as the force is coming from the centre of each subject. And the last thing in this topic is that there is also other units to measure the Force like dyne, pound-force etc. So with this our Force topic is finished now we will lear about mass

Mass

Mass was first refered by a great physicist, astronomer, cosmologist, mathematician and also refered as the father of modern science Galileo Galilei. He was the first person to refer about gravitational mass while doing an experiment. So now we will discuss about the experiment that was done by Galileo to understand mass. So before many centuries there was a thought that the more the mass, the more the speed from a particular height. Like assume that there are 2 masses Mass A and Masss B and here Mass A is greater then Mass B. Then if we will throw them from the height Mass A will reach earlier then Mass B to the ground. Then to prove this wrong galileo drop two different spheres of different masses from the Leaning tower of Pisa. And then the conclusion he gt was both the mass land at the exact same time from the height to the ground. This proves the previous observation wrong and help us to understand the concept of accelaration due to gravity, which was same for all objects on the planet and does not depend on the mass. And today the formulae that we use to calculate accelaration due to gravity is '**$g=GM/r^2$**', where g is accelaration due to gravity and G is the gravitational constant which was given by Sir Issac Newton and M is the mass of the planet and r is the radius or the distance. And the unit of accelaration due to gravity is ms^-2. And our scientists have calculated the accelaration due to gravity with the help of this formulae and it is come to be 9.8 ms^-2. And Mass is a physical quantity and does not matter whereever the direction is, it would be same. And Mass is a constant quantity and cannot be destroyed. We have also learned this throught a law which is Lw of conservation of mass, that states that mass cannot be created nor be destroyed. And the unit to calculate mass is kg. And also there is a queston in our mind that ***'What is the differece between mass and weight?'*** So i will tell you some points about the difference between Mass and weight. So Mass is a scalor quantity and Weight is a Vector quantity. And Mass is constant whereas Weight is variable. And actually mass is the amount of matter the object have whereas weight is just an amount of force that the planet is putting on us. For example- If we will go to mars, our weight would be different as of earth as thre mass of mars is way lesser then the mass of earth so if we would go to mars our weight would also be less. But our mass would be same. With that our topic of mass is also finished and now we would go to the physical quantity accelaration.

Accelaration

Accelaration is the physical quantity that was given by a great scientist Sir Issac Newton. He refered about this on his 2nd law of motion where he gives the formulae of Force that was, F=ma. It was the first time someone has mentioned accelaration in some formulae. So according to Sir Issac Newton accelaration is when someone put ann internal or external force on some object have some mass and it changes its veleocity. So now we will understand that with the help of an example. Assume that a man is pushing a box having a mass of 10 kg and he puts a force of 50 N in it and the box was at rest. Then will there be accelration caused? Let's check it out. So we know that accelaration is something change in velocity, and now we have put a force on something that have a non zero mass so according to second law 50 N=10 kg * a now we will transpose 10 kg towards left hand side and we will get a to be 5 m/s2 so here if accelaavity alration is caused then there will be definately change in velocity and vice versa. And in the previous topic of mass I have also discussed about accelaration due to gravity. Does gravity also produce accelaration? How does it do that? Is it important for us? Let us answer all your questions. Accelaration due to gravity is denoted by the symbol g. And is caused by Planets depending upon there mass. An with the help of this only we are able to calculate our weight as Weight is equal to mass time accelaration due to gravity. And also there are 3 equations of motions that were given by Sir Issac Newton. They are-

1) $v = u + at$

2) $s = ut + \frac{1}{2}at^2$

3) $v^2 = u^2 + 2as$

So these are the three equations of motions and they can also be used to calculate accelaration. And in these equations v is the final velocity of the object, u is the initial velocity of the object, t is the total time taken, a is the accelaration of the object and s is the dispplacement/ distance of the object. And also, Accelaration is the vector quantity and the unit to measure accelaration is m/s^-2. That is all we need to know about accelaration an now we will go to the next topic of Time.

Time

This is one of the most mysterious thing ever discovered. And also there are many paradox about this topic. Like is there someone who invented time? If yes so if he/she was making it then also time must be going on. So, we cannot say who invented time and at which time period. It's obvious how can we tell that in which time period time was invented. It's totally illogical. The Only thing that we can tell is that when we started to measure time. Time was first measured by Egyptians. They use a device known as Sundials. This device was found 5000 years ago. So now I will explain the working of Sundials. This device consists of a thin rod, and this tells the time using the shadow of the object that is caused by the sun. And as the day progresses, sun moves acroos the sky and that leads to the movage of the object's shadow also.

Calculating Time by Newton's 2nd law of motion

So can we calculate time using Newton's 2nd law of motion? Yes we can do that, let's see how. Newton 2nd law states that Force is directly propotional to mass and accelaration, that we have discussed earlier also, so the formulae is F= ma, and as we can see that there is no 'time' in this formulae. Now we will recall our previous knowledge and we know that accelaration is v-u/t, now here we will assume that the object is starting from the rest and u is 0. So after putting u to be 0 we will get a=v/t. And that is what we needed now we will put this in the 2nd law of motion.

$$F=ma$$

$$F= m*v/t$$

$$F= mv/t$$

Then we will transpose t to LHS and then we will transpose F to RHS

$$Ft=mv$$

$$t=mv/f$$

So this is the formulae of Time that we have got from the Newton 2nd law of motion.

Time is also a scalor quantity and always the same no matter where we are and when we are, and also here direction makes no sense. Assume that the time is going 2:00 PM and we are go 2 meter towards north, so is there any change in time? No there is no change in time. And the unit to measure time is we all know. We measure time using seconds, minute and hours. This is all we need to know about time and now we will go towards the next topic of momentum.

Momentum

Rene descartes, was a great mathematician, philosopher and a scientist who first described the law and principles of Momentum. He was the first one to refer 'amount of motion'. And momentum is the vector quantity and it does depends on both magnitude and direction. The SI unit of momentum is kg*m/s. And there is also another unit of momentum that can be used is Ns (Newton second). And the formulae that is used to calculate Momentum is mass* velocity. And it is refered by writing small p. And the formulae to calculate momentum is, p=mv, where p is momentum, m is mass and v is the velocity. And we can also refer rate of change of momentum as Force, if mass is constant. Rate of momentum means mv-mu/t and then we will take m common and will get m(v-u)/t. And as we know that v-u/t is accelaration, it will become m*a. We can also relate momentum with force.

Let us prove that

As we know that Momentum is equal to mass*velocity and velocity is equal to accelaration*time

$$p=m*v$$

$$p=m*at$$

$$p=mat$$

And now we know that ma is force (f)

$$p = ft$$

And now we have proved that Linear momentum is equal to force*time.

That is all we need to know about momentum to know about the Formulae, and at the last we will go towards the next topic of Displacement/Distance.

Distance/Displacement

Distance and Displacement are 2 different physical quantites, but there are some similaraities in these both that's why I will explain these both in the same part. At first we will see the similarities of these both and then we will see the differences. So these both physical quantities are used to calculate the length between the 2 points and also they both have the same SI which is metre(m). That's all the similaritites between these 2, yes only this much. And the differences between these 2 are Distance is the actual total path covered by an object and Displacement is the shortest possible path between the 2 locations. For example- You are going to a tree and while going you covered a total distance of 9 m, that is the actual path, which is distance but if you will talk about displacement, it is the shortest path to go to the market, which is always a straigh line between the 2 location and here the shortest path would be 4 m

DISTANCE AND DISPLACEMENT

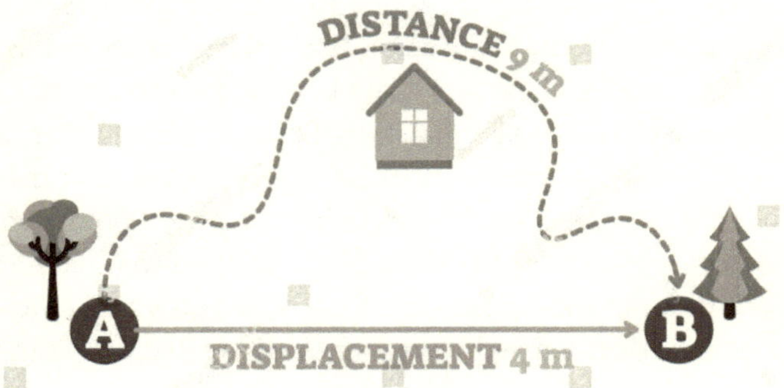

Image source- Shutterstock

There is a relation between these two that is Distance is always greater or equal to the displacement. Distance can never be lesser then displacement as displacement itself is the smallest path. But i can be equal to displacement, how? If we travel a distance in a straight line, as we know that displacement is the shortest path which is a straight line, and if we will travel in a staright line then Distance would be equal to displacement. And there is also a small concept in Displacement. Suppose that you are going to buy some vegetables foor your mother and after covering the distance of 250 m from both sides you come back to your home, so what would be the displacement? It would be 0, because the initial path and the final path is the same in this case that is your home, and the shortest path betwen the initial position and final position is itself 0. So the displacement would be 0 but if we would talk about distance it would be 500 m. 250 m for the first round of going to the market and 250 m for coming back to house. And there is also one more difference between these two which is displacement is vector quantity and distance is scalor quantity. And that's all for this and now we are good to go for the absolutely new formulae in the field of Physics. And if you are reading this, then you are absolutely lucky because you are the one of the few people that is reading this invention.

IX

The Invention

So, now we have studied all the basic concepts that we need to know for the formuale. As I told you in the previous chapter that this formulae is about the momentum. So basically this formulae states that Momentum is directly proptional to force and displacement and indirectly proptional to the velocity of an object. And if we would arrange it in the form of an equation it would look like this

$$p=2fs/v$$

This is the result of my hardwork that I have done for years and the whole story that I have told you. So now you will have many questions about this that "How did I get this?" "What is the prrof that it is right?" and many more, so I will tell everything about this formulae. So in this formulae momentum is refered by (p) and force is refered by (f), displacement/distance is refered by (s) and velocity is refered by (v) and also this formulae is only applicable when the object starts with rest, hence it's initial velocity must be 0, then only this formulae would be applicable. And also we can also write the relation of momentum with mass and time, let's see how.

So we have studied about equations of motion in the topic of accelaration, that was v=u+at and as I have said as per this formulae u (initial velocity) would be 0. Then it would become v=at and then we would put this relation the formulae.

p=2fs/v

p=2fs/at

And then we would put the formulae of force from 2nd law of motion that we have studies from the topic of force. Which was f=ma. Then it would become-

p=2mas/at

And then a and a would get cut so we will get

p=2ms/t

Now what I am going to share is the derivation of this formulae.

So at first by equations of motion we will take the value of a from 1st and 2nd equation of motion.

v=at

v^2= 2as (as u is 0)

Then we will transpose everything to L.H.S except accelaration

v/t=a and also v^2/2s=a

So here the R.H.S is equal in both cases, hence we will equate both the equations from R.H.S.

v/t=v^2/2s

Now here what we will do is put the value of time (t) from 2nd law of motion that we have found and will put that on this equation.

F=ma

F= m*v/t

F= mv/t

Then ft=mv

and t=mv/f

So we will put this on the equation that we have found.

v/mv/f=v^2/2s

Now f (force) will come on the numerator

fv/mv=v^2/2s

And as we have studied the formulae of momentum which is mv, then we will put it in the equation

fv/p=v^2/2s

And now there is 1 v in L.H.S and 2 v in R.H.S so we will cut v and v from both sides

f/p=v/2s

Then after transposing p to R.H.S and v and 2s to L.H.S we will get

2fs/v=p which can also be written as **p=2f/v**

Hence proved.

Now I have proved this formulae to you all my dear readers. But there is a problem, we all know that the formulae to calculate velocity is displacement/time but if we will calculate it by equations of motion it will not come like that. Not able to understand? you will get to know this on the another chapter.

X
PARADOX

So as I have proved my formulae and gave it in front of you, but as in the end of the previous chapter I have said that there is a problem in all this that needs to be known. So what is that, we know that the formulae to calculate velocity is displacement/time. So before going to that we will know what is the meaning of Paradox. Pardox if a type of statement that have two or more then 2 parts contradicitng each other. For example- If you have a time machine and went to past and then killed your grandfather before his marriage and came back to present, so is'nt something uncommon in this, yes. Let me explain it to you, if your grandfather is not alvie then your father will also not exist in the universe and if your father also doesn't exist in the universe then you also doesn't exist, but if you don't exist then who killed your grandfather. This is typically a Paradox. Here 2 or more statements are itself contradiciting. And for your knowledge, this Paradox is known as the grandfather paradox. Now in this case what is a paradox?

So if we will again go towards the 1st and 2nd equation of motion, and equate them

v/t=v^2/2s and then v and v will get cut from each side, so we will get

1/t=v/2s and then we will transpose 2s to L.H.S and then we will get

v=2s/t but wait...the formulae to calculate velocity is displacement/time, not 2*displacement/time.

So out of the equation of motion or the formulae of velocity, something is wrong as per the abopve proof. And now we will go towards the secod paradox.

The Formulae of momentum is mass*velocity. which tells us that momentum is directly propotional to mass and velocity. But if we will go to my formulae which is p=2fs/v, here velocity is in denominatior which means that if the velocity increases the value of momentum will decrease. Which is too contradicting the above statement. So does this also change my answer, yes it does. That's why I was very frustrated to find the solution of this but can't. Now we will look at the proof about this formulae

Now we have discussed about the Derivation ,about the formulae and also explained it to you all. Now we will discuss about the proof of this formulae. So let's start with it.

p=2fs/v we will put the value of 'p' as 'mv' and the value of f as ma

mv=2mas/v and after that m and m will get cut.

v=2as/v and finally we will transpose v to L.H.S

v^2=2as (Which is the 3rd equation of motion)

Hence we have proved that p is equal to 2fs/v. And I also want to say one more thing, in this formulae momentum is indirectly propotional to velocity but in the proved formulae of momentum it is written that it is directly proptional to velocity that I have talked about it before. So there is an invisible force that is acting on the object the make the object directly and indirectly proptional of momentum with velocity, which seems to be not posible but it is can be seen in the formulae.

XI
About book and Author

ABOUT AUTHOR

This book is written by Hiten yadav who lives in Delhi, India. His age is 14 and this is his first book. His father name is Raj kumar yadav and his mother name is Poonam yadav. He also have a sister whose name is Mahi yadav. And also have grandparents whose name are Mr. Ram singh yadav of his grandfather and Ms Shanti yadav of her grandmother. This is all abot his personal life.

ABOUT BOOK

This is a small book about an invention by Hiten yadav. This book tells us the story of Hiten when he was trying to invent something new in the field of Physics. This Book is also good for students studying in Class 9 or 10th as it tells us the basic concepts of Physics that comes under there course. And at the end he has given the formule with the proof and derivation. And he also explained the paradox that are there in this book

XII
Notes

XIII

Notes

XIV
Notes

XV

Notes